To Cu

Much love G

Pasta

P.S. Thats for

beach ball

Keeper pizza Doylon

Broken

Circuitboard

DrayZera

Performance Poetry

Foreword

You guys are in for an experience!

I've been looking forward to reading this book since I first saw DrayZera perform, just over a year ago. Now you're fortunate enough to be holding it in your hands – right now. You lucky thing.

Dray is a striking, powerful and engaging performer. His live readings are a wonderful mass of passion and kinetic energy; an experience not to be missed. This book finally gives Dray's words the opportunity to stand for themselves, stripped of the colourful trappings of performance. Now the reader can pore over and engage with Dray's words on their own merit. At last we have a publication of his works, enabling us to step inside the performer, see the soul that resides in him, expressed here through his poetry.Make no mistake, like all art, that's what you're holding in your hands; a piece of Dray's soul, extracted and refined into words. Some will bring delight; some of it may be uncomfortable to read; some will wash over you and some will sink into you, make you think and leave you changed. But it is all authentic, bold and dynamic; not for the faint hearted, the fragile or easily offended.

Dray doesn't shy from exposing the ugly as well as the beautiful; shining a light on that which others keep hidden. So be warned, it can be a challenging read.

You don't have to agree with Dray to explore and appreciate his honesty. You're not being asked to align yourself with his positions. Dray and I, for example are like chalk and cheese!

But that should never stop us from engaging with and appreciating each other's art.

So take your time, dear reader, and experience Dray's words for yourself. I know I'm going to!

Keith Sadler, singer song-writer and performer (2017)

BLACKHEATH DAWN

Blackheath Dawn Publishing 2017

© DrayZera

Blackheath Dawn Publishing Hafren House, Blackheath, Wenhaston. Suffolk IP 19 9HB

Email: enquiries.blackheathdawn@gmail.com

DrayZera has asserted his moral right to be identified as the author of

Broken Circuitboard

ISBN 9781911368311eBook

ISBN 9781911368298 paper back

This is a work of creative 'wordsmithing' and is intended to entertain, maybe shock, but definitely inform. In no way is it intended to defame any person, living, dead, or fictional. For more information on the author, http://www.drayzera.blogspot.com

Table of contents

Acknowledgements

I thank my parents Parvin Haque and Syed Nurul Haque for all their support in my 27 years of living! I must drive them up the wall with my continual arrivals and departures to perform up and down the land!

My thanks to *Poets In Motion Poetry Collective* for undying support! They are Katrine Solvaag, Shakes (Chay Graham), Roxanne Carney, Piers Harrison-Reid and Gill West.of course, despite the lovely Clive Oseman, who helped greatly, leaving the collective shortly before publication of this book.

.Love and admiration to Alex Vellis, a performer helped me to progress,and I call her good friend.

Keith Sadler wrote a beautiful foreword and this singer-songwriter has been a source of strength.

Further acknowledgments

Dean Atta, Neanderthal Bard (Stefan Gumbrell) Lewis Pratt, Ron Booth, Nathan Dean

(the *Lincolnshire Outspoken Poets* Scene plus "ArtIsntSexy" Fanzine.)

Much love to the amazing Alexandra Chambers for the artwork; a beautiful soul whose work made me immediately say "YES, I need her art in this book!"

Adam Booker for being a bro, alongside my friends Rob Gridley, Clark Turner, Ryan Butters, Lottie Gilsenan and of course by best friend of 20 plus years Dan Pettitt!

He's one stellar dude! He rocks! The wrestling community of Brett Meadows (Damien), Dann Read, Alec Burnitt, Emily Read, Folakemi Lawal (Voodoo Queen Amarah) Marc Wheeler (The Banker Mark Lloyd) and Ashley James Deering (Ash Draven).

If it weren't for Terry Gilbert-Fellows, Linda Perry and Melissa Joy, none of this would be possible. Sending all my love to all!

DrayZera (Umor Haque) Summer 2017

Broken Circuitboard

Mind cannot compute,
All in disrepute.
My sparks are gone,
All undone.
All I want is to function.
Armour has chinks,
Just cannot blink.
My world has sunk,
Loading stunned.
I need fixing please,
Virus and diseased.
My CPU corrupt,
All abrupt.
Reboot me,
Anti-virus,
Free my mb.
Wipe my drive clean,
Termination complete

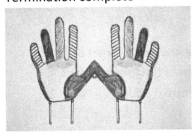

Debut

Clap, clap, clap, I feel the crowd,
"Yeah, yeah, yeah" the chants, so loud.
The clock's ticking, my hat's a flicking...
It's showtime!
"Ladies and gentlemen,
are you ready for some spoken word poetry?"

The speakers bellow as I enter the stage.

Live, at not just any old club...

The Hunter Club!

Arms in the air, smiles, they don't care...
To experience better than my first time!
Difference is I didn't pay the hotel; hell...
Well she turned out to be hell...

But, ahem...

Yeah, first time performing,

With partying and don't forget selfies!
No matter where the journey leads,
No matter where it ends!

Don't forget where it began.
Because it's where it begins,
That makes all of this the absolute best,

Thank you, Hunter Club

God Vs God

You insist you kill in the name of the almighty.
But understand whilst you sip on your grand demands of
slaughter,
There's a father, son, daughter and mother all in scarred
squalor.
Whether you worship the compass pointing north, south,
east west,
No need to strike pitiful blood, shed in slanderous valour
To follow the ancestral steps of Lent, Ramadan, Hanukah,
Divali,
Put down your weaponry before unleashing more misery.
It should not offend you,
How can acclaimed Holy scriptures destabilise you,
In what hemisphere do you sink your hate?
Why does it seethe with the rancid stench of the believer?
You know it's true.
To galvanise the disciples to wage mayhem upon the
innocent,
To systemically decimate all for twisted genocide.
To corrode the *once dreamers,* with salivated cyanide.
Humans are not classed by measurement, race nor
sexuality.
Let them love whom they want; just stop your resentment.
Stop all the disgrace and disgust!
When the rubbles over, cries of a four-leaf clover never
closer.
Battlefield blasphemous in divide and conquer with your
brushed off stains.
Yet father, son, daughter and mother will never find a home
again.

My Breasts, My Rules

What's the matter?

> Her child needs feeding.

Why aghast?

> Her child needs loving.

This outrage due to an act of nature,
Descends into a culture of mock and ridicule.
Ridiculous to think that a bond so special,
Be judged upon the locality of her breastfeed.
So what if the child is fed in the park, a pub a bingo hall,
before two little ducks are called?
This is not exposure, not explicit, no act to incite
promiscuous minds in the foolishly blind.
No one has the right to say no to love,
No one has the right to say no to joy,
And no one, no one has the right to deny a child its
blossoming bond.
As the righteous women will say all true,

> That it's "My breast, my rules" all along.

Petal

You know who you are,
You're a petal of angels.
Let me see your heart.

Frozen Socket

These volts no longer connect the synapse,
Shutting down due to overheating relapse.
Over and over, the cooling fan stutters its rotary cycle,
Stoma to coma, frequencies of voices envelopes new rivals.
Cavalier, trotting mightily through valley and over hills,
Until I spill upon my fearing chills, collapsing, shattering the
once shimmering chandelier.
This is how it feels to be a frozen socket,
Your emotional locket busted,
Your physical self mistrusted.
Staples pinning you down loosely,
On second hand paper; no one helps as you bleed
profusely.
Perhaps that's metaphorical, but the theological methodical
mindset of the mass, who treat mental health like an
afterthought.
What's happened to support?
What catalysed this abhorrent act? No olive branch with
supportive rope to give them hope.
But no, we say nope as they gurgle on prosthetic bar soap,

They smoke away their futures; hope you choke
This is not just poetic verse to divide,
Rather we reside, hide away from love, as they're filtered
by the ashtray.So don't dismay, come out to play.

This though is not a game.

So let us all plug and tighten the earth wires to neutral.
We become all snug in full connection.

(Previously published – **Poetry Rivals** 2017)

26 Miles.

Twenty-six miles, forty two kilometres

The distance between my heart and yours.

Upon arrival to your arms so serene and sweet.
With each sprinkle of the hourglass spreading oceanic shore,
Droplets of tears formulate streams of fears, forever soar.
Why? Why should a kiss bring a semblance of worry?
How? How can an affectionate embrace rain ash clouds?
You see when emotional rapport within a romance that envelops our hands,
Our words, adventures, snapshots of delights of our days and nights.
Embodies a world we formulated, crested by the seeds of our intergalactic space, and of course, your beautiful grace.
They say distance makes the heart grow fonder.
Upon yonder, 45,766 yards, 137,298 feet. The arithmetic, imperial, metric irrelevant.
Because we could paint 2,602,600,026 million miles and still my beats flow all wholesome.
We could inhale opposite planetary systems and exhale differential musical anthems.
I crush on Backstreet Boys, you dance to Busted instead.
There's always something glorious about these beautiful boy bands... Mmmmmmm.
Twenty-six miles; pages of unlimited smiles and aisles of our blossoming memories from aisle one to pristine beyond.
I'm forever blessed for you to have chosen me,
Allowing me to live and ascend all free.
I promise sakura petals to shower your unrivalled beauty.

You, yes you, erase all my staccato, holding your being
breathes new legato.
It may be cliché to say,
As the marketing media continues to spray without delay.
But from the bottom of my soil,
To the glistening skies of our well-oiled sun,
I'd like to end my piece,
And bellow from the top of my cello lungs,
To you my calming peace.
I love you.

A stray, Bull, Caged!

All I want is love,
Warmth, shelter... Just... A genuine hug.
I am not a monster,
I breathe, I beat... I have feelings.
Many stray away from me,
Why? Because of the name tag of my breed.
You know me as the pitbull,
Or perhaps... An associate that you feel deserve to rule.
You treat us as 2nd class citizens,
Preferring the pedigree as your rancid mission.
Abandoning us from shelters,
Ostracising us to make ourselves better.
Despite your amendment,
You still prefer the death sentence.
You want us dead despite rife gun laws fucking your race and world-wide rape submerging humans to disgrace?
You want Lennox killed based on his breed yet turning a blind eye to his kind acts?
If it were a black man you want dead based on skin then aren't you a shitstain racist?
All we want is love,
Warmth, shelter... A place to call home.
We will forever bark and bite for equality.
But we need you to save us all,
As all dogs matter.

Crafting Your Sacrifice

Four walls are my only friend,
As I strum these notes to the end.
Weeks on the chord bars,
Now on the pentatonic scale so far.
It's loud, yet quiet.
Staccato and legato,
Tortoise but the hare.
Jubilant, however, in despair.
Image becomes secondary,
Due to acoustic amp primary.
No need for new vans,
What does it have to do with my plans in any case?
Let alone any new haircut trends.
I'll just keep my split end mop my friends.
Friends? Did I just say that word?
The subject matter, itself non-existent, not heard.
Is this my key to happiness?
Where would my friends be if I'm in distress?
Is this my platform to stardom?
Who would I call if there's no friend at all?........ I'm
doomed.
Ahhhhhhhhh! I keep repeating myself, friends..... friends
friends friends friends ....friends friends................
Are they? Are they really?
Do they really trust me?
Why do they keep me on a leash or attempt to derail and
tease?
Are my friends the hollow tin or my friends' pathetic spend?
Is to love my friends or is my heart belonging to my string
ends?

To have both is improbable,
But by no means impossible.
Time to play guitar, with my mates...

Balance me on a tightrope before it's too late.

That Garish Lighting

Oh dear, oh dear, oh dear.
This will not do! Oh deary me.
Is that mahogany oh so grainy?
Is that decor really dour and poor?
And that ash carpet?

Oh God, just rubbish!

I need to lie down,
As I drown my sorrows and frown.
I guess that garish lighting's okay,
Oh what am I kidding,

I'm in dismay!

A Silent Dream

I look to the stars,
Gazing afar.
For I can't scream,
A silent dream.

The moonlight howls,
From the midnight owl.
Nightmare's a fowl,
As I throw in the towel.

I look to the stars,
Gazing afar.
For I can't scream,
A silent dream.

The heart runs cold,
From the icy folds.
My life can't hold,
Befuddled and sold.

I look to the stars,
Gazing afar.
For I can't scream,
A silent dream.

The voice burns dry,
From the poisoned fly.
Alone I cry,
As I tread on mines.

I look to the stars,
Gazing afar.

For I can't scream,
A silent dream.

The broken gun,
From the hollow sun.
Chasing's no fun,
To bestow and run.

I look to the stars,
Gazing afar.
For I can't scream,
A silent dream.

The wheels of fate,
Spring from spikes of hate.
It's never too late,
To pull my weight.

I look to the stars,
Gazing afar.
For I can stream,
My beautiful dream.

Vanilla Cocoa

So creamy, so dreamy.
The vanilla white chocolate hammers me erect.
I mean the milky juices swim me afloat.
No matter sourced from cow, goat or almonds,
It sprays me all over. I really like white chocolate you know!
No matter which coffee shop I embrace,
I demand white chocolate in my horny mouth!
I need to stop describing my girlfriend like this,

For The Love of Gabrielle

Beautiful, she's beautiful.
The way she walks, looks and feels.
Blissful, all blissful.
Pulls me from darkness,
Brings me to brightness.
Ascends from my depths,
Descends to sweet peaks.

Magical, all powerful...
And yet she's but one.
A shooting star, a loving sun,
The miracle seeded in my heart.
She forever will blossom and bloom.
Blissfully, beautiful,
Gabrielle

The Bench that's Never the same

I sit on this bench today,
Gazing upon the masses walking by.
Some without even a flicker, without a care in the world.
Some though, have minds fastened, minds locked, shackled
and glued... glued to this bench.
That is me, with the chills of the air embraced.
The air claws my back, strangling each vertebrae.
Why... why am I stuck on this hollow bench?
It creaks, unsafe, reeks of insanitation,...
I'm disgusted at myself.
Why day in, day out do I allow myself to collapse, into dust?
Severed; severed by those I thought loved me for me.

For when reality bites, they use me for their marionette
games.
But do not fret my friends, today I sit on this bench again
and feel shivers turn to warmth. reeks be sturdy and the
reeks sweet scented.
I am enlightened,
I am who I am.
I am home.

Breeze of the Sweet Blue Sea

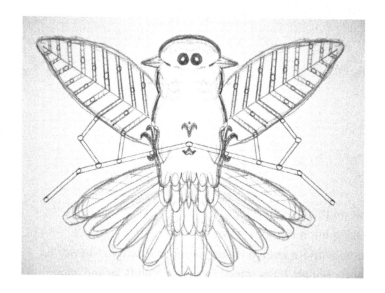

The breeze over the sweet blue sea
Light sails shine bright through the night.
Dressed in the mess, no such stress.
Let the waves sway, let it play.
Sort the claws out, loose and stout.
Climb up the mast, not so fast!
Let the fresh air bless your sense.
Dress your lip tips for the ship.
Light the wings and let it sing!
The breeze over the sweet blue sea,

I'm free.

BDSM

Us sadists are stable,
Dominants, submissive, top and bottom.
Do your research before you label,
To fist me correctly you must study my rectum.
Submission does vary,
Limiting to one's perspective isn't blissful.
The media shuts the door to many,
To not learn the ropes or whips is shameful.
Dominance takes meetings,
Consent and chatting formulates the strategy.
The safe words, debriefs are needed no condescending.
The world of bandage is no tomfoolery!
Living the kink life is fine,
So what if we enjoy the pain and masochism?
Dripping candle wax on my balls is quite divine,

This is the true story of BDSM.

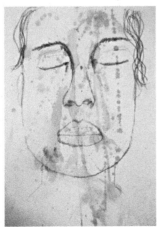

Transition

Baby born, cries,
Little boy taunts,
Teenage kid drinks,
Young adult works.
Transition.

New father stressed,
Middle age churned,
Elderly drained,
The gravestone turned.
Transition.

We are born,
We grow up,
We get old,
We all die.
But we make the script in between.

Our dreams, self-esteem,
set the scene.
Spin our axis, let love access, grind the life test.
We are in transition.

Shallow Arrows

Hey dearest, how are you?
You're so pretty... how can I ever be as beautiful as thee?
I mean it! Just look at you, It's true!
Hmmmm... Hmmmm... Hmmmm.
It's time to play the game that has no sorrow:

The game of Shallow Arrows.
It works like this! So people get the jist!
I get all that plastic,
Best foundations,
That oh so divine lip gloss,
Oh let's not forget mascara! *Gasp*
Woah woah woah! Wait!
You mean to tell me it doesn't work that way? How strange!
I mean how come you're so popular?
Getting all the handsome men;

that's mmmmmm spectacular!
By being... yourself? Ha ha ha ha ha!
Ha ha! I just can't stop laughing I'm sorry!
You mean to say I should stop copying you and enough of
my worries?
Wait... dearest ... me... In the mirror. Look...
I'm smiling... I'm spooked!
Maybe I should love myself; get my head out of the water
for sure!
And smell the fresh air of what's most important right here!

For I shan't bother anymore.

Voltic Chronic

Voltic chronic, where's your tonic?
Voltic chronic, where's that logic?
Flop flop, drop to stop.

Why must truth, leave you stroppy?
Voltic chronic, why the face?
Voltic chronic, stop disgrace.
Waves waves, stop the play,
Why can't you just, leave with grace?
Voltic chronic, voltic stop it,
Voltic logic, voltic tonic.
Logic states that you're corruption,
Tony Blair you should face treason.
For your inhumane killing season.

Snow Sakura Vs Plastic Paper

Recovered from the paper cut yeah?
Only takes a few minutes to stop bleeding.
I'm still spilling my flesh over you,
But for what? To dip your tramp Shaft to. Open lakes filled
with your heartless cum?
Give me a break, why should I cry? For each tear I shed
you're gonna make out with tongues deep whispering
"You're the one for me baby" to the next poor sod and the
next and the next for their fuckin bods.
You recall the permanent marker letter you wrote
promising me sakura petals?

Well, you proved that nothing is permanent so you can
shove your gunk of ink straight up your diarrhoea ass!
I am better than you'll ever be,
And guess what, I've stopped bleeding ages ago
you bitch!

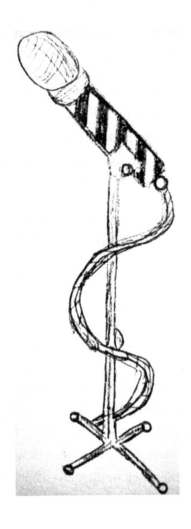

Care Cut

Life support is gone,

Imagine saying that to a loved one who desperately desires their parent, child or best friend breathing once again.

Nurses, support workers, care companies doing their best but they're forever bereft of breath abreast austerity and absurd complexity of government cuts.

Cut funding for more hospital beds,

Cut allowances for care packages instead,

And while they harp on and on like a broken record without discord they say; "we need to save, our NHS, it's great for heaven's sake!"

Well mate let me bellow from broken cello; services are in disarray down to their bone graves; nothing gets shifted from your "intelligent" cabinet.

Hospitals are shutting,

Community centres closing,

Staff stretched, surviving...

Surviving on scraps of lightning because lightning...like lives never strikes twice.

Treat care like data; numbers may not affect you personally with your congenial expenses,

Yet statistics, specifics, logistics don't support the masses.

The masses that need love...love...love...love.

The support and love before their loved one ends their life all without care so numb.

Dodecahedron Side Chicks

Lucy's tits are the best,
But my day's Gemma's ass; 'tho'...leave out the rest.
They're not free so gotta message Susie... on WhatsApp.
"Hey baby, when you next free?" x x x x x x... x sent while
having a crap.
Missed a call from Natty who's lush, let's hear this from my
delicious crush:
"Oi you bitch, you've been talking to Cassie again. You
flippin' bellend. How many times have I told you to stop
with the dick pics you sick – "
Delete! No need for that message to repeat.
Just noticed Bethany's still in bed.
It's 09.45, she gotta leave my pad by ten!
I got Kathy comin' soon after, need to leave soon so I can
clean our mess quickly.
I wave goodbye as she leaves through the back,
Start to wipe her juice slack, the front door knocks.
Kathy can't be here, God, where's the towel to cover my
cock!
"Hello?!" As I buckle under fish eye lens, shudder to find it's
actually Jen.
"One moment!" Dressed faster than Usain's 100 metre
sprint; Face so sweaty and tinted.
Because Jen's a snoopy loopy, time to delete text message
logs ahoy!
Get rid of Casey's, Abi's, Lacey's convo.
Otherwise I'll be in trouble yo!

Especially with her whips and wax strips...kinky minx.

Open the gates; I'm expecting sex, she bears rubbery latex

Pushes me to the sheets whispering, "I have a surprise for you."

Oh baby, I'm gonna strike it lucky as she pulls my pants down, ready to salivate my crown!

"Ow! Fuck, thanks very much why so rough?"

"Because you better get ready for the threesome; bet it's not enough you slut! "

"David Raven, let's get this party started!"

A voice from afar, steams in like a shooting, slinged, angry bird star...

"Jessie! What are you doing?"

Then an almighty scuffle, muscles of anger like you're on Spotify Shuffle, can't find your tune; then flush your laptop down the loo!

I got blackened and blue by my side chicks... it actually happened.

So I got left bare in full despair, realised I focussed on condom wear more than human care.

Take it from me as I cough up blood,

Don't get yourself stuck in mud.

As my twelve faces I led them on,

Don't leash them like puppets, they'll unleash you back so stop it.

Treat them how you want to be treated,

Not like meat cleavers; so don't get twisted.

Love from the heart,

Not from your horny boned shaft.

Might as well take your manhood apart.

(M.A.D.) Make America Dead

Make America great again,
Said by a hateful shit stain.
Bleeding red states unleashes pain,
Sorry America, there's nothing to gain.
Donald Trump and your twisted games,
To lead your empire to pitiful shame.
How can the electorate be so lame,
Their new president misogynistic, racist, sadist hall of fame.
Wake me up when America is great...in vain.

Fred

My libido on fire, desire on incandescent wires.
Send me a dildo, any sex toy for my holes.
Sorry for the graphic image,
I desire an orgy-filled pilgrimage.

Fuck me 'til I'm tired,
Rump my steak well done, you're hired!
I'm panting, sweating, congenial;
Your dick so beautiful, magical.

What do you mean I don't give good head?
Get the hell away from my bed.
Just so you know, faked my orgasms instead...
Fred!

Spider Web's Low Ebb Fringe

Darkness dreads a relentless kind,
To bleach the rainbows from shuttered blinds.
An empty mind, blank canvas of doubt,
Concludes, a lone crestfallen valley, I shout.
"What am I doing? Where am I? Who am I?"
As the Virgin East Coast Train floor chills my spine,
Foetal positioned, hood lowered, playing it over again and
again like a game of chess checkmate time after time.

4.12 pm arrive Edinburgh Waverley,
Excited, yet still aware of misery.
Stone paths and ancestral architecture sent me to amor.
Yet atop this amor, blackened clouds of menacing gore.
Glistening teardrops fell, crouched in this telephone box,
Screaming through the line in shock,
"What am I? Why am I here? Who am I?"
Darkness descends, a renaissance kingdom,
A renaissance of bonfires in celebration of Fringe
Magnificence stardom.
For whatever reason

Whatever fate twists as of late,

I stand for Inky Fingers the first day, the 11th month one
year on,
I perform, to continue forever strong.
I am here, have no fear.

I know my ebb.

The Finest Mount

The man Mr Mount,
King Edward's finest pleasant,
Timeless fab moments.

Unfriend It's The End

Tears and tears dripped from my puffy eyes,
Hands shake and shake in frivolous guise.
My heart beats and beats in furious fray,
As Annabelle unfriended me... from Facebook.
I'm in fuckin' disarray.

How could she?! Various memories upon memories
between us from dawn to dusk.
The time she said yes to a front flash selfie under a bus,
The moment we had an engaging conversation in the
encyclopaedic library:
"Hey Annabelle, you alright?"
"Go away."
That Holy matrimony event whereby we danced under the
nightclub stars... for all of two seconds!
No idea why you said I dance... like a bellend.

The chair creaks and creaks its wooden frame,
The tele signals crack and crack during Game of Thrones for
shame!
The world's not worth breathing and living anymore my
friends,
Because she deleted me...It is the end.

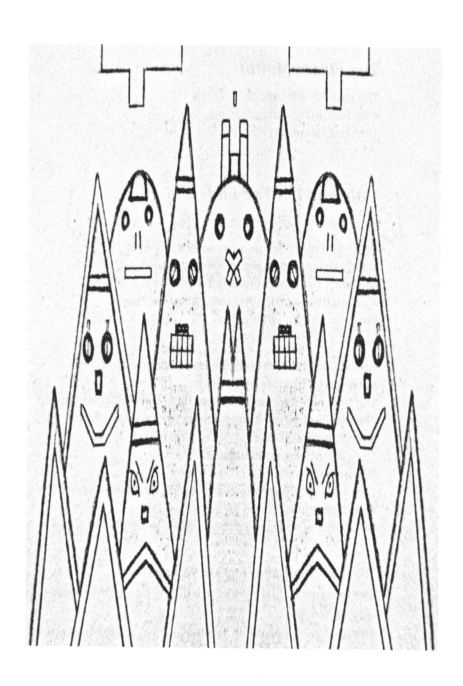

Grime In Demise

What's going on with the youth of today,
Why the bitchin and swearing? Their language of everyday.
What has happened to society?
What has happened to education?
What has happened to us.
Don't blame these children, none of these games.
All they're doing are expressing these words of misogyny,
racism, sexism and unleash them without guidance.
While thanking BG (Blackpool Grime) Media for giving them
a voice,
You claim that these artists aren't your views at all... But
let's face it, you want these lyrics and controversy to spew
for the ad money it's true.Artists Afghan Dan, Little T, Soph
Aspin, Millie B are all bright sparks but are being butchered
by the mediocrity of society's bloodthirsty stone mentality.
Leave WillNE, other Youtubers, columnists be because
they're giving you what you lust for: Popularity. Did I forget
to mention money?
Thank you especially for Will for bringing this to all our
attention as you deserve a mention. Interestingly, the mass
TV media outlets don't care to cover this. I mean heaven
forbid should the Royal Family's children embark on lyrics
with words that rhyme with ape and bigger that they get
slandered but these kids... Leave em be, does the current
government even care about the North?
What has happened to respect?
What has happened to togetherness?
What has happened to love?
What has happened to our kids?

Gin Unlocked

David is not bad I guess,
Sips gin.
Hmmmm, he has a nice smile I suppose... oh bless.
Sitting down, sips gin.
Well, his calves look so tough I bet he's walked miles.
Stands up, sips gin, finishes gin, drinks more gin.
Goodness, I never thought shoulders would flex like that!
Walk around with two glasses of gin, chugs it down loud
and proud.
My days, the way he shakes his hips. It's as beautiful as
Swan Lake, just kiss my lips.
Stutters in zig zags with toilet paper trailed by the sole,
topping up more gin.
God almighty, praise this glorious man in this presence from
head to toe he can de-robe anytime – oh my.
Slurring, crawling all fours without a drink, knocking a
bottle, throwing up in the sink.
He's the man of my dreams,
He makes me scream from my lungs,

Shivers my plump bum.

Let's have babies, maybe? Please... oh please!
Fainted, hungover head,
woke up in backyard shed.
Opened up my feelings,
But he ended up leaving.
Perhaps it's a sin,
To drink so much gin.

Dating Oh One No!

If you're going out on your first date,
Please don't state you only wash during each general
election.
I advise you to wash more often to ensure
your date stays intact for more than 10 seconds. Nobody
likes to snuggle up to repugnant bellends.
Then again, I question how Kirsten Farage lasted so long
with Nigel.
If you are going out on your first date,
please ensure you ease into conversation;
rather than barking, exploding onto stark self-revelations.
For example, stating you've had fantasies of Donald
Trump's rump... steak... whilst eating atop his lavender
chamber

May perhaps, cause an outcry and sigh of, "see you later."

Please don't even fathom the thought of discussing Brexit
before even asking their name.

Because that's quite frankly shit and lame.

Just like the red bus pledge of funding the NHS if we leave
the EU. Just... Ew.

Finally, if you're going out on your first date for the love of
all the brie cheese within my fromage scented jacket...

Don't nickname your date President Bush... as some clever
pet name for shame! Don't even validate let alone salivate
or masturbate a pro-Bush beat that goes:

"Yo, yo, yo President Bush,
He's so good like my morning wood.
George Bush oh Bushy Bush,
You think he's a bad guy sssh... You're jelly mad! He's the
hero like Braveheart but more fearful like hear his battle
cry... rawrr

Yo, yo, yo, President Bush, he's so shit not a regular 'everyday guy'. He thinks he's fly, ride the skies. I hope one day you get arrested for all your lies"!
Drop the mic.

Now, if you were to state the last paragraph first instead, then maybe you'll receive cuddles in bed instead of death stares of dread...

Because morning wood so soon is poking your far too forward exposed without even a loving rose.

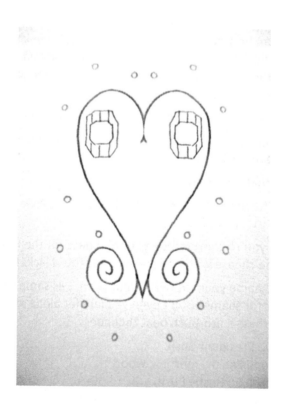

Life of a Soberholic

As I have my shot of 100% orange juice... from concentrate, witness my friend off his face making crop circles using his steaming piss for heaven's sake!

Oh... life so sober,
Oh... live the high life forever
Oh... life so sober
Forever I'm on hardcore H_2O.

As I have my second shot of orange juice... with juicy bits, in the midst of an orgy consisting of drunken hombres playing with Barbies in their plastic birthday suits.
They insisted they felt the climax despite Ken coming in doing all the ploughing. They continue to boast, saying it was amazing.

Oh... life so sober,
Oh... live the high life forever
Oh... life so sober
Forever I'm on hardcore H_2O.

As I have my third shot of orange juice... not from concentrate, I was drunkenly informed Bernie Sanders was the new President. However with resentment I disclosed to her America will never be great again. Then she waffled about building some wall...

Oh... life so sober,
Oh... live the high life forever
Oh... life so sober
Forever I'm on hardcore H_2O.

I'm out of control; downed shot four, five and six of orange juice alongside a line of Nobby's nuts on top of the toilet seat.
At least I lined it up neat without skipping a beat.
Now that's a mean feat, despite how much I've had.

As I finished my lines, my spine shivered as I witnessed a satanic drunken act on an open toilet cubicle; two individuals eating fried chicken... without washing hands.

Handed over the soap before they murdered another breast as I whispered to them...chugging the seventh orange juice... with extra juicy bits.

Oh... life so sober,
Oh... live the high life forever
Oh... life so sober
Forever I'm on hardcore H_2O.

Oh... life so sober,
Oh... live the high life forever
Oh... life so sober
Forever I'm on hardcore H_2O.

Floodline Travesty

I'm a fortunate man,

Yet what I saw in '06.

Looking back, made me feel sick, stomach in a twist, knot and kick.

Kicked, as I witnessed a game of football played in flooded plains en route between Shylet and Dhaka.

6 am, the horizon rising in the pollution of this ravaged nation.

Streets littered with insanitation, animals without vaccination. Such divide between rich and poor churned my eyes; how this world is utterly despised.

I have family below the living line, searching for scraps with the grace of my mother, donating money to their pockets to give state of mind.

This is the reality; floodline travesty, sea levels rise,

Bangladesh land erodes without reprise.

So whilst I'm a fortunate man,

There are those so fortunate

Bala Tako, inshallah ek seen afner desh batash kushi.

Stay good, if God wishes one day your country will feel the smiling winds.

Black Lipstick

I croak jealousy to these dragonflies,
The misery compiled by their freedom fluttering wings
Free to ascend in tangents with their peers like magnets,
While I choke on my bitter dose of tablets.

Pardon the ungratefulness, but my upbringing is of an
unyielding mountain.
Gradient steeper, the darkness deeper,
The thirsty lucifer quenches as I dream a wishing fountain
Dispensing narrow alleys without my shining lantern.
However, I admit of safety, starving my clean butterfly from
becoming the venomous moth; fuelled by nature's grace,
not by absinthe's marionette fate.
But what is life without some fight! What are rights with
your sundial denial,
To marry me away to a shadow I never met,
To showcase me in your spotlight without loving my sights!

Entrapment by your accursed whipping ways.
Strife I battle with scars of sorrow caused by your
lambasting slays!
So what if I'm bi, so what of my ink, so what of my
maiden tone from a world you disapprove of from your
apparent high horse!
This is my life, my fight, my right oh Mother. This is my mic,
my light, my beautiful sight thy Father.
So what of my Black lipstick? I shall fleece it with glee as
you embark on your pitiful sick!

I choke jealousy to these butterflies,
The colourful destroying my freedom's
Stuttering stings.

Free to descend like missiles honing to my painted target,
While I croak on my fatal dose of sadness
I am the marionette Lucifer, for my doll like state of lies

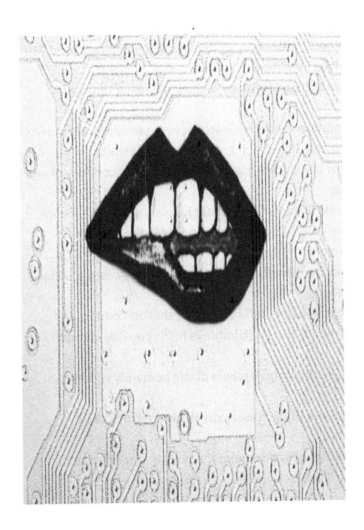

Nameless

Media outlets **(N)**ame the scene of the crime,
The reporter **(A)**nnounces the appalling numeracy of casualties for dimes.
Poisonous blood **(M)**oney seeping humanity through misery,
Thus unrepentant **(E)**vil is scuppering, tarnishing all scenery.
We become **(L)**ost in this symphony of violence,
Mouths taped **(E)**ndlessly by our voices in cacophony of silence.
They ride **(S)**eamlessly without humility and consequence,
With whispers **(S)**uffocating our fists in the name of malevolence.
The marionettes **(Y)**o-yo our minds in brainwashing under their thumb,
Handing us **(O)**ut pitiful crumbs of shallow comfort as if we're dumb. The 1% **(U)**mbrella holds equality in their grasp,
And yet **(A)**rumoured militia divide humanity without a gasp.
Millions are **(R)**elentlessly struck off the Earth like a checklist,
Tick tick **(E)**xplosions boom the skyline, smouldering to mist.
They will **(N)**ever, never, ever stop,
Until we **(O)**stracise recalcitrants 'til the day we drop.
Curses we **(T)**rample the forgotten, like market wipe out,
Selling shares **(F)**uck our rights, our dreams, we scream and shout.
One family **(O)**rders us as toy soldiers on a string,
Wealthiest the **(R)**othchilds are the sinister serpents coiling

our righteous wings.

Sadistic bites **(G)**nawing us whole one by one, believing they've won.

Bestowing and **(O)**ppressing our flesh marked by infra-red guns.

Moments in **(T)**repidation, they feast on our darkest fears,

Enlisting the **(T)**remors these Richter scales are drawing us near.

So stop **(E)**vergreen naivity in front of our doorstep,

As the **(N)**ameless will not die 'til we draw our last breath.

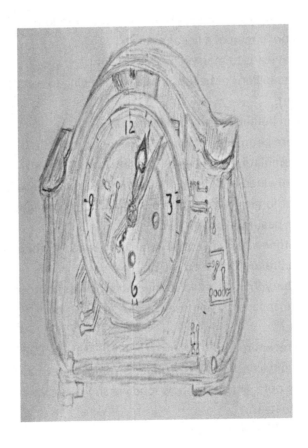

Barriers through Time

In a free flowing world of today,
They say to us, "love whoever you want to love" come what
may.
Yet, to give us that riposte without realising,
That to bury their lies through countless costs is quite
mesmerising.
The cost of expression, righteousness and freedom.
I was born a man of a linear path,
One that leads to marrying "My own kind."
Forsaken billions of beautiful souls in allowing to serenade
my heart.
How can humanity be so fickle and blind?
There are people today who are swamped in trepidation,
Love formulating between a Pakistani and an Indian.
Arms entwined by Ling Xu of China and Kazuya of Japan,
Let's not forget Post-Apartheid South Africa continuing to
divide a beautiful nation.
1969, Stonewall Inn, Central Park 78, Rebecca Wight and
Claudia Brenner... Erased in 88.
In February 97, Otherside Lounge Atlantic was bombed
because apparently homosexuality is an "Aberrant
lifestyle?"
And in recent memory Orlando of this year... The LGBT
community continues to live in fear. Yet it seems that day in
and day out... No matter how loud we shout... Nobody
wants to hear.
We breathe the same air,
We have a body,

We have... Emotions,
So why do we have commotion.
Tell me why do we have this sickening elation, this
sensation that we have to justify ourselves in loving
whoever we want, whilst in the back of our mind we raise
our barriers for the torrents of taunts?
Why do we even have to fight this anymore?
Why are those that are hell bent for pitiful scores?
Why aren't the ones in power deliverings universal love
worldwide?
Why aren't the ones in power desiring freedom for all
humankind?

Forever I sigh.
Look at my skin and tell me eye. to eye that it's a sin to love
those that I have fallen for!
Despite the apparent lore, I am a human being that wants
to love men and women regardless of colour forever more!
In a barren constellation, right now,
They say to us, "You can love, but by our own rules" The
cows.
Yet, despite the barriers through history and time,
We will stand, we will rise until the day they say to us,
"Love is universal, love is magical. Love whoever you want
to love," forever you shine.

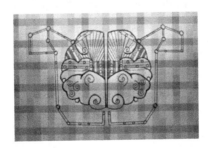

Under The Whipping Sandals

Hit me, I said hit me,
Over and over again.
I deserve it, every bit of abuse,
Springs a blossoming obtuse scarlet.
Dripping, cascading my worthless face.
I am the epitome of disgrace,
No place, no space, not even worthy of a chewed up
shoelace.
They told me once I escape,
Plight in darkness out of sight to the light.
Strips my flesh to nightshade daggers.
This fairy nightmare forever and after.
Strolling these sombre streets,
Noticing the local folk,
With streams of serenity and beauty,
Amongst family lovingly cheerily merrily toasting the glass,
Without seamlessly noticing me.
I can still smell the carcass of my sister battered by hate,
Smoulder of rubble suffocating my tears from falling.
War has crippled everything,
My life rippled to nothing.
In new land I lament forsaken,
Within this nation, all I want to some place to call home.
Because as sister's final memory was my smile,
I'll strive to find shelter, even in this frostbite weather

There is no Love: Only Turrets

Boom! Do you hear that? The sound of explosions of our remnants
This disillusion bombarding your transparent ideals of resentment!

Oh you don't know!
That's the sound of no love! It's done, begone!

Oh fun! Embrace the turrets, no sorry don't cut it!

You plagued my shrivelled nerves, crippled my mind

and tossed me to the kerb!
Just want you to know, if you're hearing my words...

Yeah you heard!...... my words...

By the way you treated me like the balls of your feet and make me reek of the lack of self dignity within my social plate of scenery...
Then, all I can say to your next victim is, let him be him, don't toss him to the bin; that's a sin...

You're better off making love to a tin!
At least... that way you're the one that's gonna feel sharp pain within your brain...

And I promise...it will stain!

Delirious in Pounds (or Kilos)

There's this new fad diet I saw on tele,
To slay the weight from my chunky belly.
They say I gotta get a China cup,
Scoop up what I can and sip like a pup.
Do this three times a day they say,
Ah yes! My lovely cherubs I know how to play!
So I go to the chippy and order the following:
Savaloy, cheesy chips, cod roe, chicken nuggets, some
scraps.
My rumble in my tum is bellowing,
As I told them to stick it in my mug!
Eh, not the foggiest why they stare at me as if I have a sick
bug.
I don't think I get this, "healthy lifestyle" malarkey,
Okay chappy folks stop being snarky!
So a week after dieting at the local chippy and "Weight
Watchers" meals,
I weighed myself; gained one pound!
That's 0.454 kilos for you lot metric and sound.
I did my jumping jacks and star jumps,
And even told Darren to grind me more humps.
I'm in disarray... my chunky belly's here to stay!
"Hold up there!" Who said that?
"It's your conscience called Pat... wearing a hat!"
"What do you want Pat?" Why the bloomin' hell are you
wearing a hat? Makes no sense!"
"Shut up you sixpence and listen! If you want to lose
weight, enough with the delirious act and start being

serious! Eat less, move more, drink water. Enjoy life! Now
chuck the China cup away and have your say!"
So I chuck the China in relief,
Shouting from the rooftops in belief,
"Yes, I will do it my way! I shall love my bloaty body!"
So from now on if you're worried about your weight;
Wait, relax and slimmer simmer down as you'll be a weight
loser!

The Discord Of Witchcraft

Pitchforks sharpened sulphur rust
Tears invalid fears inferno.
Cauldron spitting acid of no trust,
Stiffening rope coils to choke.

Scorn disinfectant burned on treason,
There are no reasons.
 Bleed unrepentant turned to ashes,
Pulverise the lashes
 Discord Witchcraft

Curses you took my Mother,
Misogynist bullshit you cattle us dry.
To live for centuries the 2nd gender,
Shrouding the mist to black tar skies.
 Scorn disinfectant burned on treason,

There are no reasons.
 Bleed unrepentant turned to ashes,
 Pulverise the lashes
 Discord Witchcraft.

Did the holy slaughter tell them to die?
Were the rabid rampants ordered to kill?

Did the holy scriptures scar their eyes?
Or was it the masculine supremacy.
 Scorn disinfectant burned on treason,
There are no reasons.

Bleed unrepentant turned to ashes,
 Pulverise the lashes
Discord Witchcraft.
Fight you feminists.

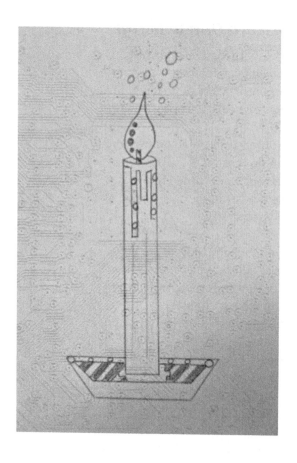

Leave the Porn Stars Alone

Oi you with your condescendence,
Bewitched of malevolence.
What gives you the right to chastise these stars?
Just because they bang and flick,
Help Jack and crank their dicks,
Embrace their vagina glands; no don't be sick,
You're the bugger with your head up your arse.
Leave the porn stars alone,
Let these porn stars groan.
You there with your sinister scowl,
Shrouded by musky towels.
Why the hate for those thrusting so hard?
Because they enrich their careers by climax,
To swap bodies and pummel profusely to the max,
Bareback pleasures spreading love in the sack,
As you're the bugger with your head up your arse.
Leave the porn stars alone, let these porn stars groan.
Why the shock of Asa Akira's soapy massage?
Or the seductive gasps of Cory Chase's whimsical passage.
To shame and outrage at Nacho Vidal's masturbation,
Are those that pour kettle to Johnny Sin's bountiful
erection.
Because you're the bugger with your head up your arse!
Leave the porn stars alone, let these porn stars forever
groan

3 Line Vape

Did you know I vape?
Smoking circles with my cape,
Shut me up with tape!

Outlaw in 105 Words

Shotgun splits the air of trepidation,
Shivering perilously shakes checkmate sensation.
Crack of dawn absorbs the descendant,
Crimson cries cascade on my fiery elements.
Treading torturers enlisted by the law,
Tampering our minds to poison us all.
Seeping seductive poison concealing blatant facts,
While my light desires to stay intact.
Divide and conquer to cement distress,
Churning castaways aside in bleak street addresses.
Stretchmarks, body hair, double chin cries,
Shaming, slandering those that love their bodies.
Torches twist hearts coil to blame,
Compiling their sorcery with their sickened games.
Be the outlaw you always wanted,
Teach these government bastards they'll be the hunted.

Realisation

I believe I have to end this chapter.
Because nothing lasts forever
I cannot be on my final tether.

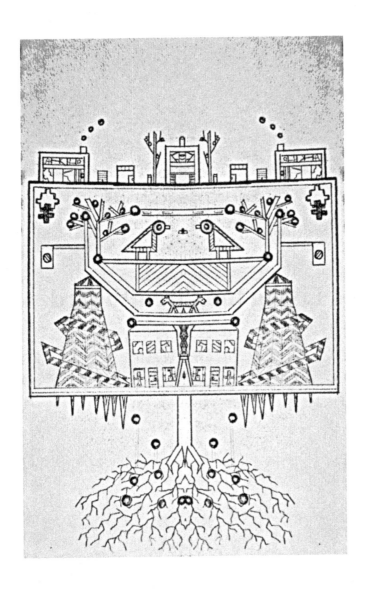

59

Fixing the Circuitboard

11

Tasered Spirits

Torn, shrouded tourniquets, stumbling trumpets,
Sultans twisting, screws tormenting sunsets.
Trashed scrapyard, torches spring twilight,
Salted tongues slither tranquilised sight.
Tripped trodden tales, twisted terror,
Scorn solvent sails, severed soldiers.
Truthful tirades translucent to trident,
Scathing scabs scar skies sacrament.
Tactful trolls tinkle, trunks, the satanist,
Sinful suits sabotage selflessness to selfishness.
Trained suits twists soiled truths,
So trounce these souls to tasered spirits.
Turned slingshot tarantula surfaces toxins,
To suppress tinned screams, tears surrender.

No Disability

We all have ability,
There is no disability
You cackle and tease,
But there is no need.
What gives you the right?
To label and write.
She can't do this,
He can't do shit.
Just because he has Downs?
Or she has what? Dementia?
Deafness, blindness, dyslexia, dyspraxia, ADD, Aspergers,
VPD, epilepsy.

The shallow group them low,
But the deep trust and know.
These are beautiful souls.
Like you and me, with goals.
Goals for a better tomorrow
Despite the shallow hollows.
Hollow and stuck with their tricks,
Tricks that should make you sick.
Because disability or not,
They are strong willed; so stop!
For there is no disability, so rot!

Instagram Vanity

I am fabulous,
Filter me pretty.
So marvelous,
Take my pictures silly.
Worth golden karat grams,
Selfie scenery.
So like my pic on instagram
Or I'll shower you with misery

Instgagram Vanity
Instagram Vanity
Instagram Vanity
Instagram My Vanity

I am gorgeous hun,
Flash me in 4K goodness.
My curves on point this bun,
Enrich this moviestar priestess.
No matter artificial,
Or Natural light.

Give up, I'm magical.
I know I'm pricy don't fight.

Instgagram Vanity
Instagram Vanity
Instagram Vanity
Instagram My Vanity

Filter me pretty.
Take my pictures silly.
I am gorgeous hun,
My curves on point this bun,
Enrich this moviestar priestess.

Instagram My Vanity

A Saturated Crowbar

Forty-five grams of fat atop this metal sheen,
In turgid crumples this once deep clean.
This is the tale of the saturated crowbar.
The once oiled machine that opens without a sweat,
Has ended up a washed up room to let.
A value once of seven or platinum eight figures,
Plummeted to a 99p rusty cheeseburger.
Carnival confetti followed sharp footsteps of gold,
To dried up wings of the icy crow of cold.
This is the tale of the saturated crowbar.
Seventeen years from the abrupt tour in Asia,
A wilting prybar stood atop the open mic stage.
Ready to perform because fuck all the haters,
Unleashing the inner rod within prime rage.
"Sent to me, these stains of rain.
Lords of pain that sets me free,
From the shackles you laid.
From the heart you enslaved
And I... "
The crowbar snapped in two as the tune collapsed,
The crowbar realised it overdosed on Prozac.
Yet with its wits intact, he snapped his hat back,
Hobbled up and confronted the devilish cackles.
"None of you know me but don't give a shit,
Because despite nearly two decades my flame's still lit!
Headlined in Glasto, Rock Am and the entire globe,
You all snipe me like right-wing media, get choked.
To all majesty and ministers that coils all sinister,
Wash your morbid cutthroat mouth with Listerine.
This is my renaissance of this crowbar bitch!"
As the crowbar exits the stage,
Despite being trampled, snapped, dusted and battered.

The saturated crowbar is no more,
As his legend lives on forever lore.

Santa Slays

Santa slays, Santa slays,
Slaying to dismay.
Oh what fun it is to bribe,
In a broken 'ciety.

Hey, Santa slays, Santa slays,
Slaying to dismay.
Oh what fun it is to lie,
In a promised cold wasteland.

Santa slays, Santa slays,
Slaying to dismay.
Oh, what fun it is to cry,
For the presents emptiness.

Hey Santa slays, Santa slays,
Slaying to disgrace.
Oh, what shame it is ostracise,
On humanity's destruction.

The Autumnal Rise

These darkened nights, surrender my light.
Moonlight so bright, sunshine denied.
Under these fallen leaves,
Gripping air chills a freeze.
Lies a damp crust disease,
Mud wilting down to my knees.
The autumn rise, must conquer your prize.
No more lies, live before you die.
Why do you shed a tear?
How come you live in fear?
Can't you shift, change your gears?
Break your mind thou shall sear.
The autumn rise, must conquer your prize.
No more lies; live before you die.
Rise from the root of denial,
Lies wretch, your eyes are defiled.
Prize seeks ascend to greatness,
Die not defy your tempest.
The autumn rise, the autumn rise, the autumn rise, the
autumn rise.
The autumn rise, must conquer your prize.
No more lies; live before you die.
Fight 'til your last breath, dance 'til you fall on your
deathbed.
Life is too short, don't abort, don't deport.
These brightened nights, sunshine alive
The autumnal rise.

The Man Who Ran away from Fixing a Cracked Screen

Phone cracked,
Lost my mind.
Oh my God,
What to do?
Found a man,
Fix the screen.
I said "cheers",
Passed the gear.
One week passed,
No phone still,
Confusion,
It's stolen.
Mother said
"I'll sort it,"
I pleaded:
"No! Don't mum!"
Oh my God,
What the hell.
My downfall,
Is blind trust
A coward?
Feels so hard,
For his act.
Rest assured,
I am sure.
You will soon,
Lick your wounds.
As the tale of the man who ran,

From fixing a cracked screen disbands.
Realise all those who believe you decipher,
All you are is a liar.

Jigsaw My Heart

10, 000 pieces jumbled, tangled in this myriad Web,
Chamber all jagged, sharpened boulders pummelling my walls.
A casting downfall of emotions revoked and plastered again and again,
Piecing them all in circulation; such a beaten dead dream.
I scream from left ventricle to right atrium,
Scribble my clotted arteries unto requiem.
Nothing makes sense,

My inner aorta bleeds of repentance, malevolence and beguiling cadence.
Became a sadist tranquillised, ostracised, demoralised, crucified,

For having feelings.
Buried deep within me, beats in searing heat,
Lies a tepid soul wrangled in defeat.
The day my pulmonary, tricuspid, and mitral valve shut down,
The moment I crown myself the drowning clown.
I am not an emotion that functions by light switch,
Nor a plastic flesh that's someone else's bitch.

I am my own jigsaw, no more, no less, embracing my own core.
Sure it's a chore to go to and fro to what fits in part,
But rest assured, the map from inferior to superior vena
cava... The pathway to my own beating heart

Sexual Oil

Oh yes baby yes! Pour that blood oil down my neck.

All over me!

C'mon all over my corrupt body.

I give you the green, you build your machines.

Create the war you always wanted

....And make it sexy.

Bring Cameron, bring Putin!

Hell; bring back Bush, so he can sweet honey fuel baby between my legs of chalice.

.....Because while I keep pumpin',

I'm a gonna' keep killin'.

Sexual Oil II

Oh God baby no! Oh God! Get your poisonous brick
outta my dick!

Please go away! C'mon this putrid war is making me sick!

I stand on front lines, you load gun with lies.

Versed to kill 'em all

.... And make it dreamy!

Afghanistan, Iraq, he'll bring on Syria while we continue to spray our bullets into their blood lustful oil.

'Cos while they keep on cashin'...

I'm a gonna keep on slavein'!

Shush Tubes

Ssssssh, be very quiet as I leave Platform 3,
To hop from Central to Hammersmith and City.
Snuggled in my headset, my own universe,
Along with commuters shackled like me.
This carriage alone bears stacked sardines in tetris lines.
The chundering stuttering of the shuttle tube slices the
silence of bubbled masses.
I pop the bubble by switching off my tunes,
At which I witness the zombies full of disconsolate thought.
Pondering, surely this lot can't all be introverts,
Has social media swallowed us whole?
That solemn soul bears a wristband from my favourite
band,
A conversation is something I must conjure and muster
before the bewildering shush gets out of hand.
"The next station is Mile End, change here for the District
and Hammersmith and City Line."
Had to shoot off before I said "hi"; whine inside and sigh.
I plug back my headphones as soon as I step out of this
human centipede
To Hammersmith forth to Stepney Green,
Repeating the arduous underground journey and
amalgamate in complete sssssssh.

Upside-Down Pyramid

I dream of becoming the greatest crème brulee of the
entire galaxy.
Feast on me my pretties for I am the answer to unholy
misery.
Suck it up as this salty caramel is ready to annihilate,
Decimate, destroy the destruction caused by the ravenous
snowflakes.
For Heaven's sake, let me bake off crisp full of oozing juices
please,
I'm the magical fairy not so hairy taste me to tease.
Do you not know my name? I'm the colossal legacy,
scream it out loud and proud "The dessert of ecstasy."
Don't think you understand you desolate disease,
For I bring forth order by my custard cream.
Don't tame me by rules and salty whips,
I always fly from my landing strip.
Bastards heed at my battle cry,
Otherwise thou shall all die.
My pyramid upright,
Stop being so tight.
No priorities,
Dead worries.
No crown,

None.

The Don Queen

"I dreamed a dream," a famous phrase said by a champion
of justice and might,
Yet this phrase can be extrapolated to various fights that
bring forth mellifluous delight.
2006 Soapbox was born,
500 plus events later, continues its incandescent form.
From open mic beginnings,
To festival blessings.
A tranquil romance of spoken verse,
Unravelled unto a collective Communit, cuddled and heard.
Many performers; Novus et Veteris say grace,
Thanks to you, dearest Don Queen.
As within these walls bow to you Amy Wragg,
You championed a dream into reality.
Spoken word is forever alive!

The Poetree Walk

10 am beckons ladies and gents,
As we tread along upon the fields abreast. Here we have,
Bards Aloud, bestowing upon his poetry.
Oh my heavy winds, his words all so flowery.
Along with Matt, Tom, Karen and everyone else,
We're having a jolly good time, oh yes!
This represents togetherness,
Resonates majestic bliss.
This is Folkeast,
A weekend of creative feasts.
So let us all glow and show to all the valleys,
Our artistic gem shall remain completely happy.

Hamlet Again?!

Walking down the town witnessing a poster.
I noticed a familiar title,
Hamlet again?! You absolute fuckers!
And it made me frown in anguished ire.

Now I know Shakespeare's a lege in this globe,
But if you haven't explored world theatre,
Do I have to pledge to shout in your lobe,
To see past "King Lear" and spoon and feed ya.

Embrace Ferguson's show "Fat Girls Can't Dance,"
Enjoy the breakneck "Bull" by Mike Bartlett.
Check out Bohemi's "Who's The Daddy" once,
There are other programmes you poppets!
Exam boards, elitists and linear cakes,
Tune in to other plays for heavens' sake!

Counting Down The Material Pearls

20,000th in this queue,
To acquire something new.
Something material,
Of this cauldron I skew.

7000 left,
In the middle of this test.
Credit card sharpened,
The battle of the best.

Hundreds to go,
Nerves jangling my glow.
It seems this queue has faded,
Time to enter the show.

Upon entering discount twirl,
I gripped this material pearl.
Noticing I spent hours so static,
For this plastic stop-gap I curl.

Why do we budge by the big bucks,
Just our luck they suck our humility astray.
And we pay and we pay til we can no longer stay,
In our home stuck upon this crippling snow-dome..

LinkedIn Description

I am a passionate performer of poetry and such,

which I love so much, with eccentric delight

from sunshine so bright to dreamy moonlight.

Forever I dazzle with entertainment

without going out of touch.

My objective, to make people happy

instead of being crappy,

To continue living the dream of performing

in front of joyous screams,

And of course to make the world a better place

without the disgrace of corruption to embrace us all.

Let us all be creative,

Let us all be abrasive.

Let us all be LinkedIn.

Through The Flowers of Denial

Through the flowers of denial,
These fluorescent daffodils defiled.
Breathe in the tranquillised air,
Limbs dangling upon the cliff-edge despair.
Wilting leaves crackle the soil.
Rising tensions surface to boil.
Hailstones shatter my convex bubble,
The sandpaper etches my mind of stubble.
Slanderous lies wretch my soul,
Nothing to stabilise me, lo and behold.
One day I dream of pastures melancholy,
And nobody, and I mean nobody.
Shall diminish my story.

Quicksand Orbit

When planets align, gravitating to the sun.
Continual orbital co-stellars foretold you're the one.
The beating arteries circumference, apparent love.
This amor unravelled unto a limping dove.
Once fluttering its pristine wings,
In incandescent vigour enchanting songs, dance and joy
reigns upon blackened sand.
Coils in my neck,
Brains empty led.
Voiceless, I bled.
A hole in space,
Repentance shattered piece.
Distasteful snake you never cease.
Thank you for the darkened enlightenment

An Alternative

Should I stay or should I go?
Should I suck or should I blow?
Oh my goodness, oh these decisions.
Should I walk or should I run?
Should I muffin hard or cream – pie bum?
Oh my goodness, oh these decisions.
Buy a house or purchase a flat, what should I choose?
Swallow whole or spit out her cat juice?
I need to stop choosing pornhub.com after work
Otherwise there's no alternative but to give my dick a twerk

Today

After our first kiss,
Of blushing bliss.
Each day since,
It's you I deeply miss.
To be honest,
Ever since I gasped my first breath,
Lost in your poetic words abreast,
My heart beats, skips;
Especially upon enshrining your lips.
My feelings are strong,
I want to hold you for so long.
You've opened the gates to a world I belong.
Your life. I'm alive. I cry.
Why do I cry you ask?
Because today, tomorrow and future days,
I can tearfully shout in joy.
You're the best. For you make me smile.
In jest, sun shine and fully blessed.

A pathetic Meteor

She broke a nail, her life will fail,
As a thunderous meteor will prevail.
She lost her straightener, annoyingly bitter,
But the imperious rock will beat her.

She cried because Sammy forgot her money,
However, the inferno of the boulder's not funny.
Mum and dad didn't want her to party,
It's all so close now that all will be bloody.

The lipstick snapped,
The sky cracked.
Her Myspace's silent,
Meteor vigilant.
Her shower's cold,
As the ball unfolds.
Her eyes saw fire,
Situation dire.
Meteor burn, burn, burning, sizzling,
Excuses, excuses...

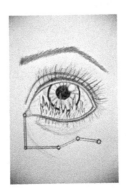

A Pathetic meteor returns

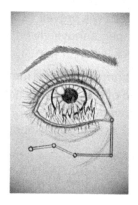

She smudged her brush, her mind is crushed,
As the demonic Meteor serves you a crunch.
She stole extensions from mum's precious pensions,
But the boulder shall scythe without a mention.

She blubbered because daddy said no;
Yet incandescent flames of the rock will show.
Stephanie forgot to do her nails,
As the atmosphere cracks your smouldering fails.

Her foundation gone,
The Meteor shone.
Her Facebooks no likes,
Melting in fright.
Her selfie's no filter,
Furnace on kilter.

Her voice cries for love,As life goals are blunt.
Her plastic world evaporates,
The situation too late.
Meteor burn, burn, burning sizzling.
Open the door... open a door.

#FreeLauri

Dear Mr Cameron and Mr Obama.

Why are we here? Why all this drama?
Do you not understand?
Why don't you understand?
What don't you understand?
When will you understand?

As long as a Murdoch has pies in the holes of number 10,
You might as well smell the dish of reality in the
Whitehouse! The end!
We have here a man that wants to spread his wings of
love to beyond and above.
But all you desire is for his heart to be shoved under your
poisonous gloves.

We stand before you,
Not superheroes, not corrupt MPs nor snake-like senators.
We are true,
Stuck as glue.
Not even firearms can stop us going through,
For the truth.

Set him free, like the breeze of the bees
Setting the love pollen in glistening glee.
Set him free I say Mr Prime Minister and Mr President.
#FreeLauri

Marriage of Two Tongues

When we walked down the aisle,
The tears streamed down mother's cheeks.
I saw your face stern and demure,
For the rest of my life, we are destined as one.

When we had our bodies entwine,
The warm embrace turned damp and cold.
 I saw your manhood infiltrate my insides,
For the rest of my life, we are destined as one.

When we had our first meal,
The candlelit evening went up in smoke.
I saw your face in benevolent disgust,
For the rest of my life, we are destined as one.

When we speak to my locals,
The barriers and mannerisms are best left desired.

I saw your eyes spraying in venom,
For the rest of my life, we are destined as... What are you
doing to me?!

Let me go, I said let me go!
Stop! My tears are already streaming down both cheeks,
Your face so luckier, not even God can crucify.
I thought the arrangements brought joy,
Yet a sickening ploy by the Lord.
My ribs and my heart is broken with discord.
As my spirited mind and soul lies paralysed by the sword.
For the rest of my life, we are destined as dust.

Sulphur Sadness

Rotting rancid reptiles,
Disgusting disciples.
Putrid plastic people,
Oppressing oiled oceans.
Nature nears nuclear,
Castrated coal clear.
Forest flames fierce,
Environmental ecstasy.
Tears turn torrential.
Mercy maniacal.
Sulphur servitude,
Sulphur satanic,
Sulphur seduction
Rotting, disgusting, putrid; oppressing nature.
Castrated forest, environmental tears of mercy.
Save suppressed system.
Sulphur sadness.

Blindfold Nobody Asked For

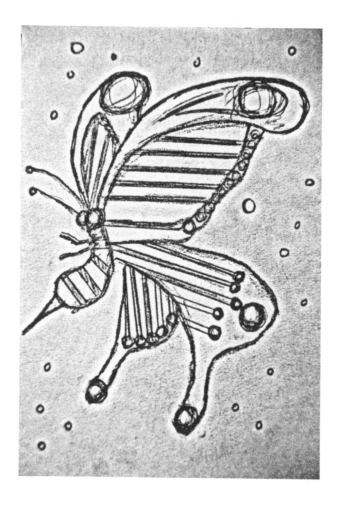

The path that guides me collapses to mud,
warped dimension grinding knees to a crippling thud.

Body murmurs at times, yet rattles violently,
unto my basket of solitude that cracks open profusely.

The warm, familiar voice allows me to unwind.
Yet it manifests to a heretic demon, supressing me inside.

Everyone loves me, yet no one understands me.
Surrounded by love without moans, yet forever alone, I
groan.

I surround my being with beautiful butterflies.
But why does it gnaw and sting without surprise?

This cold sea boils kettle,

The sky is upside down.

This gourmet meal tastes of metal.

The air is making me drown.

My pallet is empty,

My paint so plenty.

Why is the light dark,

Why are the smiles stark.

Bed of Nails,

Blissful sails.

Angels Sail,

Devils Nail.

Pain,

Love.

Rain,

Doves.

Pain,

Love,

Rain,

Gone

Cause and Deflect

Deflection: The art of denial.
Destruction: Malice Revival.
Twisted circles, misty hurdles.
How do you do it?
How can you do it?
Breathless lies and candid eyes,

Why did you do it?
Why do you do this?
The grips of the mace,
That you shovel in disgrace.
I shout mercy,
Yet you ignore without say.

What is your reason?
What are your reasons?
Play the game without consequence,
Pound the nails within my severance.
Why? What? How?
How? What? Why?
Why... Why... Why...
Deflection: The art of silent effect.

Destruction: The vicious cycle of cause and deflect.

Rifle in My Trifle

Smoke this cigar sugar,
'Cos I'm quite promiscuous
So delicious, not religious,
Fill those lungs up with tar... baby cheeks.
Stench, hungry big trunks at the bar,
Thirsting on me like some dolled up porn star.
So revolting, just disgusting.
'Cos I'm some easy slut for fishing.
Serving for nickels, hurting so fickle.
Tossed from skin to skin like a rag,
Too many bullets from rifles,
In my trifle... so much so it's turned to a gag.
Us dames suffer from having breasts we stifle...
Thrusting out of delicacy
Throbbed into misery.

Holographic Harpsichord

Sparkles, serenade me please!
For I am worthy of my destined glory,
Appease my forehead cretins that tease!
For I need my body to be fanned; understand?
End of story.

Do you see my magical mansion?
Have you witnessed my scrumptious Italian?
No not the food silly! My magnifico man!

Damien... such a dreamy, creamy, hunky, cheeky monkey!
But listen ladies, he's no flash in the pan... catch my drift?

Ah lookie lookie at that rainbow just born!
What's that with wings? A unicorn?! Wow!
Okay is this air real?
Or is this just some sick ordeal?
Why is my mansion... peeled?
Wait that's not right? Damien? Oh Damien?
Damien... a rod just got him reeled! What's going on?
My sparkles are gone!
I just fell asleep.
Forgot to pay the bills, again, eep.
My debt is so deep.
Why did I let it go so steep
Shit.

Jester Joker Juggles Joy

Jester joker juggles joy,
Casting cuddles courting coy.
Letting lumber leashes loose,
Grinding grapevines garbage goes.
Jester joker juggles joy,
Poking pancakes pouting pugs.
Yelling yanking yellow yolks,
Trying, toiling tearful talks.
Juster Joker juggles joy,
Beauty, bravo. He's our boy..

Fried Of The Rising Sun

Ohaiyo sweet Nihon,
The fudo so amazing.
Crafted with passion,
Yet so much fried food! Baka!
Nazedesu ka? Why...
Everyone enjoy fudo,
Hai...ie it's true.
The fried of the rising Sun,
We're more equal than we seem.

Love All,Not The Crimson Falls.

No chew toy, nor discarded bling.
Then why must those who oppose true feelings,
Be the ones who forsake and dispose little sap
trees.
Sap trees born in blatant homophobia,
Grow and blossom,
Petals and fettle
Climb and triumph in blissful utopia.
The utopia birthed from our powerful voice,
All of us, lesbian, gay, bi, trans and straight rejoice.
For crimson must forever stall, let us not fall upon
the pitfalls and call.
Call from our hearts and let it beat true...
Love us all, love for all.

Violate My Teacup

You! Yes you sir have violated my tea,
It's not as pure as it used to be.
Why must your people invade our land?
We have enough trouble in our hands! Be banned!
It's not as if we caused chaos before,
Creating casualties and gore to the fore.
Well... there was that airstrike once,
Perhaps that other invasion on a hunch!
Wait, wait! You mean we violated their tea too?
Hold your horses that can't be true.
Perhaps, "weapons of mass destruction" were never found.
That's kinda dodgy, doesn't it sound?
This is planet Earth after all,
We do breathe the same air for sure!
So to protect our own,
We must build all teacups a home.
For we must grow and save,
For humanity's sake, tea needs to be made.
Cheers for the beautiful brew.

An Uncultured Sponge

Soak it all up Mr Sponge,
Yes people drive the other side of the road,
There are people who use chopsticks,
Let alone those who eat with their bare hands!
You think that's bonkers, mad?
Well it should definitely make your head spin ie people
chuck powdered colour over one another.
You're crazy man; well I'm not.

Because I have the trump dare that will churn you oh so hard!
You heard of the Kanamara Matsuri festival?
You haven't? Ha, thought so!
It's in Japan; wanna go one day you uncultured sponge?
That's the plan!
Well you're on your own; it's a penis festival, au revoir mon frère.

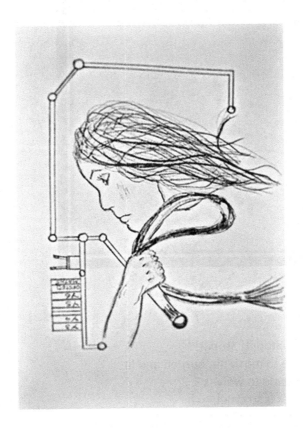

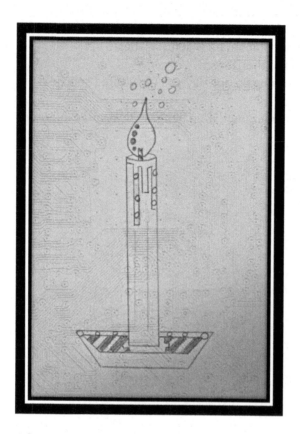

The Flame Within Me

Stop it! Stop it! Stop it!
Cast me to mosh pit, burned and lit.
You fed me to wolves,
The pack is so cruel.
Chewing me up inside,
With no one by my side.
The pain, the stain, remains.
Piranhas gnaw my veins. Cold and rain.
All of you doubt me,
For my wish to be free.

To stand on my own two feet,
Singing harmonic beats.
Ascend, arise, within!
You believe it's a sin, to rise?
To ascend from the pack,
With my heart intact.
Punch the sky with venomous might,
It may cause a fright.
As the embers inferno,
Be truly in my key.
I can finally breathe,
In the brightened eve.
The flame within me.

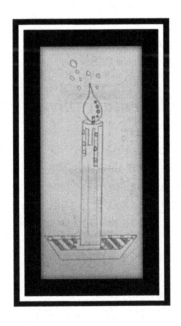

Holi-Yay

Last shift before the leave,
Bags packed, ready for the breeze!
Check in,
Boarding.
In plane,
Excitement of course remains!
Landed,
arrived,
To begin my Holiday, yay!
It's finished,
Reboard,
Back home...
Bloody hell, back to work; groan!

...With Complimentary Olives

She dumped me for another man,
Told me my inches came up a little short.
Her new partner is...Well perhaps was my best friend...
What got me most riled to the hilt with my kilt,
Is that she still has my hoodie...With complimentary olives.

Taylor Swift released a new track,
Bizarrely it didn't mention any exes.
Her lyrics were "I love my feta,
More than Mona Lisa. Can't beat the beat,
Can you feel the heat."
What got me most perplexes is that she mentioned Mona,
the heat and feta cheese...But no complimentary olives.

My Mother told me I was adopted,

Weas told my parents disowned me on the Jeremy Kyle Show,
Despite DNA tests, no Christmas cards or triple chocolate birthday cake.
I never received my complimentary olives though through the post.

I then had my 11th birthday (wooo!)
Adopted Mother said I can have "Whatever I want,"
So I said to her - My true family, my friends and my Cat Hermoine all smiling...
...With Complimentary Olives.

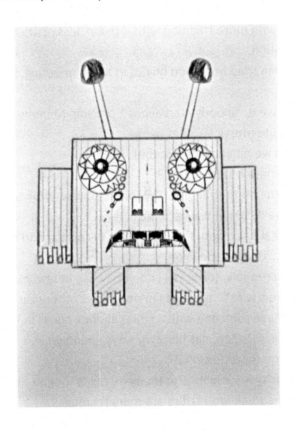

What's Authentic?

Now I refuse to go to India,
Not because I don't like it...you heathens!
It's due to the... how you say... authenticity; so listen what's
coming out of my mouth and stay.
So obviously this poet, (yes this poet here) has that origin...
Okay guys stop looking at my cocoa skin.
So, I can vouch that my mother (of course she's cocoa too)
cooks it with more tradition with incision, less restriction,
more tuition.
Some even tried her onion bhajis, at a staff meeting, given
free.
They all went, "bloody marvellous", praising Mummy Zera –
an absolute must!
But then we hit another diatribe!
Do you know what it is guys?
What if the mother-in-law, (chocolate too that's for sure),
cooks in a different way to mum!
Yes, typical Asian film, they sort it out in combat and curry!
Yes? No... okay I'll move on.
So mother-in-law, (okay yes I don't have an in-law, but let's
say I have a wife to pretend I'm not single; otherwise I'm
gonna shave someone with a knife) ahem... cooks in her
own style, Mrs Zera has her own ways, meanwhile.
Makes you think doesn't it?
Authenticity is subjective to the taste bug's tongue,
Makes me think food critics are mongrel mugs!
Ladies and gentlemen in the room, you decide what's
authentic... all change, no static and turn the page to find

this Indian cookbook saying it's authentic and a hook
Oh boy, guess we're all crooks in need of a vigorous shook
(Cough, past tense)
I can guarantee this poem is authentic at least!
Because I've made it DrayZera majestic and you all need an Indian feast!
Don't like curry? Well... Go get doggy treats then! Now that's neat.
Disclaimer, if I've offended anyone whilst this poem was read, performed or otherwise... then I'm sorry! No I'm not! Why should I worry! Free speech, end of story!

The Tech Guy

Duct tape on wires, strapped on floor tired.
Tired drips of sweat, pressure to be the best.
I'm that guy nobody knows,
I'm that guy nobody cares.
I'm just... that guy...
Line mic sound checked, lighting addressed.
Addressed and stressed alone, falls down, fails, only me to
atone.
I'm that guy everyone snarls at,
I'm that guy everyone glares and spits at..
I'm just... that tech guy!
Performers on fire, crowd arms raise higher.
Shifting the fade, my life is made.
'Cos, I'm the glue,
'Cos I'm the unsung hero, it's true.
'Cos I get up early, coffee shot.
'Cos I set up from dawn, untying knots.
I never signed up to be the man.
But got thrusted into, trusted, with the plan.
Makes me feel congenial,
For which I smile within my tree.
Branching out from gig to gig,
Smoking cig to cig – perhaps in stress.
But gotta do my best, otherwise the show's a mess.
Just another day.
For the tech guy.

(L.O.T.S) Lord of The Shaft

We have... The Eiffel Tower,
We have... The leaning tower of Pisa
We then have... The Taj Mahal
"But wait, that's not really tall!"
But you know what's big, lo and behold.
The mighty shaft of Adam Booker
Mighty as the thunderbolts of Zeus,
Tougher than the head of a moose.
My goodness when you wrap it hard,
Joysticks already in fifth gear – in charge.
The power, the glory, trunk and holy.
Bow down, open to the top of his crown,
As it thrilled and pound, steamroller and proud.
From the plateau IV 1 novice,
To the champion IV 40 climax Prince,
To the ejaculatory IV 80 demi-God of glory,
As when it's over... all this tells the story
Of Adam's mighty... Penis...Of Man!

Is Ginge the Captain? Really

He thinks he's the captain,
But he's better at shittin'
Oh Gareth we love you!
He thinks he's the captain,
But he's better at Guinness
Tipsy after one pint,
Can't even fly a kite,
Banter Princess! Banter!
Oh Gareth we love you!

Unsalted Caramel

It doesn't taste the same anymore,
Because... I guess it's just a bore.
Rich salivation, turns to plastic stations.
Bland is just the understatement.
It was gorgeous at first,
But then I lost the thirst.
Perhaps my life is cursed,
My mind and my purse.
Why does it have to change?
Why do we have to shift?
Why can't it taste the same?
Perhaps I need to leave my box,
And try one, maybe two flavours on the trot.
Strawberry? Apple? Blueberry?

It's time to sweeten the mind.
To the cherry stall I go.

Forbidden Fruit

Bite into this apple,
And it opens up...
It's dark, damp cobwebs,
Shackles the goodness within.
Now when the fruit bears radiance,
And you go deeper,
And deeper
And deeper.
You see that it's all forbidden.
Why oh why? Cry oh cry!
This is what I get for bursting into this blood valley.
Bleak and bleak and bleak.
But then... an awakening arises.
The air freshens, lifts me high; so much so I don't want to
die.
Despite the dangers, despite the fears and despite all evil.
I'm so glad I fell in love with you.

(A.P.A.M.A.P)

A Poem about Making a Poem

Do I put peace with cheese or peace with crease?

...Aaaaaaaaah!

God I'm so shit at this!
They're just gonna take the piss aren't they?
It's just I write these words,
And I wanna be heard but... but nah...

Anxious man!
Why the hell would you wanna hear me talk about politics?
Or religious fanatics?
Zombies? Werewolves? Ummmm... mummies?
And I mean mums like Ellie and Jessie!

Not them dudes wrapped up ha ha ha!
Anyway where was I? Oh yeah yeah, poems!
Reading it out is like, unlocking your bedroom door.
It's all access to the fore.
I can write deep

like gore... whores... my dog's paws... see!

Personal stuff from my brain of fluff!
Wow... That sounded so cheesy!
Ah yes! Cheese with crease! Perfect.
What am I worried about? It's my life after all.

Wait that last line doesn't rhyme...

Screw it! My poem, my rules... baby!

Scars Beyond The Pines

Forest bears these scars of mine,
Treating them so kind, eyes drained and blind.
Leaves rattle my cage of rage,
Pages and pages of battles engaged.
Sometimes I try to blend,
To hide in my sheltered cave to mend.
Cast aside by fresh branches of oak,
Letting me soak under this deluge I choke.
I keep telling myself each day of mine
Time and time again until I die,
That my scars Beyond The Pines,
Tells the tale, a story with all its deep cut lines.

Dear Nurul

Your heart may have black,
Attached, with impact.
But alas, you stood by me intact.

Each passage brings forth pain,
Drained braved, with stains.
And yet! Did your best albeit in vain.

Why in vain? Well let me say...
Our landscapes are different,
Despite bound by name

Our philosophies opposite,
Despite bound by blood.
Our worships breathes paradoxes,
Yet we bear the same flesh.

When you departed, a piece of me ruptured and cascaded.
Because, despite the phantom menace you brought.
All I can say is... thank you, dad.

Bearings of Seven Billion Eyes

I stand, view. Breathe the air,
Air shared by the masses.
I sit, rest, bring all in,
All in the furnace, the flame of my mind.
And when I rise,
I despise and reprise.
Reprised by the eyes,
The bearings of seven billion,
The pressure... No leisure

Innocence (pt.1)

Modest claps brought life when "Angel" was announced
As, with Acoustic Guitar set, came to their sound.
This ebbing stool of wood awaited her company
And she accepts, all to the misery of its creaks and
murmurs.

The simmering silence descends down to Angel's crowd,
For her heart felt the derailment of the "should-be" proud.
Her naked right limb etched and itched to her new blue
symbol,
A tear, spelling out beneath, "Forever I weep."
She locks the memories, "Thank you everybody,"
A glass of liquid ice soothed her throat.
"Hi, I'm Angel, and I'm going to play a special
Number for you all; Innocence."

Then, the modest claps then battled with cheers,
Angel's right woven with the fretboard.
Creaking again was the stool, in unison with her tapping
foot,
Young Angel's head bobbled up and down in the Melodic
rhythm.

A hushed imperious quiet accepted Angel's opening,
Fluttering generally with strings one and two close to the
hole.
And then, when the chords slowly made its mark,

Her lips, mouth heart and soul poured itself out...

Innocence (Pt.2)

A decade passed since "Angel" debuted the stage,
Accompanied not only by acoustic guitar, but also backing band.
"Angel and her wings" The full ensemble,
Selling and tumbling records slaying artists they tremble.
Blossoming in Rhos On Sea to superstar in New York City,
Angel's life has escalated to new heights beyond delight.
Posters, billboards, airplay - The full buffet.
The light and stars are in full alight,
As the premiere of "Angel and Her Wings: The movie" is in full swing without delay.
Suddenly, dehydration and sleep deprivation has caught onto Angel upon the red carpet,
As she collapses head first, paparazzi encircles the fallen Angel like sharks in detonation tanks swamping...

Why?

Why does it have to be this way?
Why did I do this?
Why did she leave me?
Why? Why? Why?

Why must I go on suffering?
Why can't this pain go away?
Why am I the monster people say?
Why? Why? No!

I am not a monster, why?
I am me.
I am not suffering, why?
I am free.

I am not in pain,
You ask why?
Because, I lived the life to be.
I am free.

The Recipe of Life

Rules are in place,
Work, law and games.
But, a recipe of life?
It's not the same.
Nobody told this banana to grow,
Let alone said to ducks to feast on bread.
Funny, no one tells us about nuts and bolts – all that shit.

It's as if I gotta read a whole rulebook... but it's impossible...
Impossible...God dammit I'm stressing out...

Give me tissues someone? Anyone? I'm in turmoil!
Rules aren't in place,
Mess, aches and loss.
But, a recipe for life?
Guys, we just gotta wing it... because we... we are the key
ingredients... each of us.

Chicken And Noobs

"I'm a teabag you!"
Fatality,
Just another noob bites the dust.
Another boss battle,
Oh if I must.
I chomp on that damn chicken,
While I'm the Mothertruckin boss
You're all at a loss.
No matter the cost,
I'm the elite class,
With chromium armour,
I have the power!
And then it lags,
Router crashes and sags.
They may have taken my mmorpg time,
But they will never take my succulent chicken whilst
I'm alive!

Valentine's Game

Welcome to Valentine's Day.
The day where hearts are plastic,
Value of millions, – no actually billions.
Don't you find this all a game? Well do you?
Let me ask you something;
What does a box of chocolates do to your romance?
Does it really mean anything?
What about taking them to dinner? Pay for their meal?
That's nice, but will it really kindle your love?
Love... love isn't once a year, it's three, six, five days; twenty
Four hours and each hold, squeeze and embrace.
Each and every loving minute of tender, love and care.
Valentine's Day is not the 14th! It's every day, forever and
after.

One

Born in a town of white majority,
With its colophony of history.
The past shunted minorities
Ran them out, to isolate.

Growing up under a different tongue,
breathing another world within my lungs.
About to dismount,
I scream and shout.
Shout at the divide,
The divide broken by our eyes.

Living in this world with decisions,
With its earth ironed out by religion.

This planet blighted with politicians,
Corrupted, dismantled with delusions.

I learned to love
People, colour, all of us.
As we breathe the same,
Born as stray lambs,
What comes after, unplanned.
So don't play games,
Let us all unite... as one!

Horses and Bunnies

I'm so, so tired,
But I just got hired
Hired into what exactly?
Well... hired to hop onto Ellie!
Ellie is a horse!
I heard she's a chore.
Well... such a chore I'm frightened!
But on the saddle,
It's no hassle.
Hassle free... her hair bristles in glee.
This is the life,
I have the fight!
Fighting them bunnies... lack of batteries.
Yeah, I referenced Duracell,
Yet my fears... can go straight to hell!

Secret Life of Devon Anderson

People want money for ease,
But they don't want to be me.

So let me tell you the story son,
The secret life of Devon Anderson.
I was down on my luck,
Just couldn't give a fuck,
About people, about prospects
'Bout life to be honest.
But then I scrolled the Web,
And found the name of Seb.
Owns an agency of sorts...
With a plethora of escorts!
Three Fifty an evening without even sex,
And Four Fifty plus with? This is the best!
And despite the sins, plucked up my chin,
Registered myself at elegence4her.com.
Say goodbye to respect it's gone.
Been told to build my portfolio,
So I can cash in on them filthy holes.
Build up the client base,
And live off an alias.
Swap the bodies in a flash,
And sweep the whispers in a pan.
This was to be my future,
But son, you know what happened after do ya?
I bottled my first job,
So I still got a virgin knob.
You know what son? I only wanted to share,
Because there's new worlds out there! Beware!

Mother's Prayer

This is the first birthday without her in sight,
Perhaps this is the part of growing up,
But yeah, she's gone to dad in an emergency,
So each day, within myself, I recite this prayer :
Nearly Twenty-six years with your prescience,
Yet suddenly disappeared in abrupt fashion.
In an impoverished country – Bangladesh.
Where you reside, I grow each day with worry.
But I know you'll be safe, yet it's been a struggle with each
passing breath I take.
I guess like a mother's prayer, you always wish to have your
children sheltered and respected and cared for.
All I want for you is the same,
And I hope you come back soon.
I love you mum
Amen.

The Earth in All of Us

(Written by DrayZera and Ellie Bear)
We are upon this soil,
Living this life through curiosity and wonder,
Upon which the sky clouds pour their rain.
Love and light, we reach out to pain,
Towards something which remains.
This is the Earth in All of Us,
Beating our heart of which we trust.
Living a dream that we once dreamed,
Upon a bountiful castle we cried and wept.

On this earth that's part of us and with us,
In creations within, we are enough.

Kick Out at Two (Squared Circle)

You know that feeling
1...
When you're on the edge of the seat... And
2...
And when you think it's over, suddenly...
"And he kicked out at 2! How... HOW did he do that?"
Perhaps it's to the script, but I care not one bit!
That adrenaline... the drama... the movie-set, laid out in a
perfect cake!
(Provided booking is par, goodness sake)
The tempo, the suspense... all its atmosphere!
Week in week out, they lay their bodies on the line.
1...
For your entertainment, aiming to amaze, despite their
spines.
2...
And when it's over...
3...
You applaud and chant for both wrestlers
Years of craft happened not fast, but with heart...
Apart from their loved ones,
Away from home,
But to find a new space,
To taste heel to the face,
Bumps and pains; hurts like a mace.
Is this squared circle, owned by you all?

Tribal School

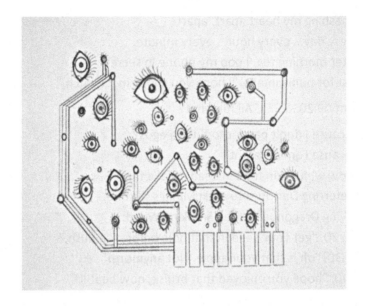

07.45 am, got woken by mum,
08.00 rise from the bed,
Leaving behind my messy solitude.
08.15, soggy brekkie done,
Leftover spag bol from last night.
"Let me stay, let me stay mum please."
By 08.30 it's too late,
Another day of twisted fate.
Unconditional hate.
Billy no mates; tribal school.

"What you looking at freak?"
"Stop looking at Becky! You're too ugly anyway!"
"Where's your daddy? He never loved you!"
The growing tribe barks its barks,

Smashing my heart apart; apart.
Every day... every hour... every minute.
After morning reg, I pop my phone in secret,
Just for punishment, "I hope you choke in P.E bitch,"

sent 09.20.............All for what?

Because I don't pander to fluffed egos?
Because I am different?
Snow white skin tone instead of fake tans,
Preferring Deftones to Nicki Minaj's silicone,
Loving Dragonball Z than Smoking Weed.
10. 20, "get your head in that hole before we flush."
12.30, "oh is that your apple. Not anymore!"
3.40, "hope you enjoyed that bruise, now beat it!"
Is it no wonder ten years on, I'm still strong?

Why? Tribal school is dead, nailed on its head.
Have my own tribe now, my friends and my clean solitude.
Because never forget who you are,
Because nothing can tear your heart apart.

It's your life, your fight to newer heights.

Now that I finished.
Listening to "Back to School" by Deftones,

Time to switch off at 10.00 pm,
Goodnight.

Centurion

Millimetres from a nick to first slip,
Getting used to the surface,
Pressure as a furnace,
Still on a duck, better not trip.
Relief as the first run tickles legside,
Then a cover drive for four offside.
Took me thirty balls first boundary,
But no worry just carry on happy.
Bowler strides in, hits the deck,
Venomous whip coiled from his neck.
Call for leg before, going over thank Lords.
Thought I finished my final chord.
Sweat drips as I creep to fifty,
Strike rate low but still a plenty.
Spin bowler on, time to change stance.
Revolutions on, which way will it turn?
Read the flight, hit all its might churned.
Six! Rode my arms, blasted and chanced.
Onto eighty-seven, unlucky for some.
Final session nears, gotta gun them runs!
Oh no... out?! Oh thank Grace it's No Ball,
Ball before tea, a definite dampening fall.
But alas, I'm still in, twelve runs 'til glory...
Final session,
Nervous nineties
Scamper a single,
Nudge a two
Now on ninety-three
Rush to three
Ninety-Six

And then... relief
"Long off straight drive, fielder isn't gonna get it! He's done
it! Century off two, three; three balls!"
Take off the helmet,
Point to the sky,
High and dry.
Stumps it is.
Finally I leave the crease, bat aloft... leading the plaudits.
Media duties.
Back to dressing room,
Time to rest the bat,
Go and kip... do it all again next day.

Cackle My Efforts

What I don't understand is that,
While the English language is widely spoken,
As a main tongue, 2nd tongue or even a 3rd lick,
why must people cackle my efforts in my speaking lingo.
Okay, yes I was born here in Britannia but spare a thought
to my parents whom their jargon is a tad puzzling.
My Mother says to me (I'm translating of course) since the
age of seven,
"Son, how do you spell Pounds" when writing a cheque.
I obliged and assisted, despite this question repeating and
repeating like the rejection rate of of potential partners:
Daily (For me at least.)
However, you see...She's trying! Sure, she's lived in this
country for longer than I but keep with the cognitive and
realise that we're not all the same.

With our brainwaves, experiences and calorie intake all
as predictable as the National Lottery. Yep...Lost again.
There's an underbelly within our society whereby we
go...Ha, your English is terrible who taught you this? Get
back to school you uneducated bitch!
It hurts. It hurts especially those who's attempting to go toe
to toe with our English vs theirs so they can cope! But no,
no nope,
We kick them to the gutter without any sense of remorse.
Let me shift gears in giving you the scope that world
language is dope!
(For all non-colloquial purists out there when I say dope I
mean wonderful or amazing, not the drug.)
I mean saying "You're so beautiful" "Esti atat de frumoasa"
in Romanian sounds sexy.
"Anata wa utsukuschidesu" in Japanese.
Hell, even,
" Hai il miglior cesso al mondo! Posso chiedertene il fornitor
e?" in Italia sounds mozerella-licious. Know what that
means?
It means "You have the best toilet in the world!" Can I ask
who your supplier is!"
The point is that us Brits or Americans or whomever
adopted English as their numero uno are lucky that it's
spoken worldwide. Therefore, there's a lack of deep
intrinsic need to add dos or tres languages to our
translation CV.
Everyone else though does not have the luxury,
So don't hark on your tomfoolery.
Stick a sock in your gob,
And appreciate all English efforts with a sob...

The BroSisterHood.

Through various guises and countless hair dye,
You've been there for me.
Through sticky mountains and intrepid swamp lands,
You've been there for me.
Cracked memories of nightshade slashing my insides,
Whilst the same photograph snaps a tightening hand
supporting this scaffold.
Lo and behold our old mixtapes bring forth nostalgic charm,
Yet no matter what harm or countless scorpions stinging
our vision moving forward,
We can all dance and be merry with seductive pizza and
blissful Ben & Jerry's.
On this day I raise my glass and see the reflection and glee
of my brothers and sisters that never gave up on me,
Tomorrow I will meet new faces in stamping my social
portfolio and send it in 2nd class.
But yesterday the rose that was wilting so rotten.
To Special Next Day delivery to
become the man I am today..

The Food Erection

Written by DrayZera and Rachel Melissa Mann

To some people, food is food.
But nothing beats a beef stew.
Who'd have thought it could change one's mood,
And make me want to dance nude.

To some people, food is God,
Just wish it agreed with my bod.
I chomp on bacon sarnies in heavenly glee,
But why the fuck does my weight balloon like the seven fuckin' seas!

I'm experiencing a feeling I can't explain,
It's like a weight on me without the pain.
Lie down in fear of not getting back up,
Because I need a crane to lift up my butt!

I'm experiencing a feeling I can't restrain,
as if my brainwaves have gone insane.
I've just witnessed my unrepentant orgasm,
The wet and dreamy 12 inch meatball sub... with all the succulent ham.

A food coma is what I'm in,
It's like flying in heaven on food God's wing
I get to relax and enjoy the feeling
But oh wait one sec.... a food baby's appearing!

And this baby is named buffet,
With all its love from grilled aubergine to chicken lingerie.
Dangling it's juicy carrot within my mouth,
As it satisfies me from north to south.

And here lies this sexual mastery

My gesticulating climaxing salami.

The buffet bed orgy of tapestry,

As my food erection shoots out all misery.

Keeping Promises

Promises are important,
Hold them deep whilst awake or in your sleep.
If it doesn't damage holistic combines,
It definitely won't hurt your insides.
Hold trust tight,
Love with light.
Don't lose sight,
Keep the fight.
So let me repeat in saying that promises are
important,
So hold me tight whilst awake or asleep.
Because I'm awaiting our steamy homosexual fun,
For your javelin harpoons me from your smoking
gun..

Debut

"Clap Clap Clap" I felt the crowd,
"Yeah yeah yeah" the chants so loud.
The clock's ticking and yes my hat's a flicking...
It's showtime!
"Ladies and Gentlemen,

" are you ready for some spoken word poetry?

The speakers bellowed as I entered the stage, live.

Live, at not just any old club...

The Hunter Club!"

Arms were in the air, smiles like they don't care...

To experience that was better than my first time!
Difference is I didn't pay hotel and hell...

Well she turned out to be hell...

But, ahem...

Yeah, first time performing,

with partying and don't forget selfies!
No matter where the journey takes me,
No matter where it ends!

Don't forget where it began.
Because it's where it begins,
That makes all of this the absolute best

,

Thank you, Hunter Club

Tell DrayZera what you thought of his first book

Register for DrayZera's next book of passions, complexity and knowledge.

DrayZeracreative@gmail.com

DrayZera is coming

LIVE,

to a town near you.

http://bit.ly/DrayZeraaction

Co Host Dray & Keith's 30 minutes of nonsense

http://bit.ly/2t542wQ-weeklyshow

Member of Poets in Motion

http://bit.ly/2sflQ5E-poetsinmotion

Lightning Source UK Ltd.
Milton Keynes UK
UKOW01f2206070717
304877UK00003B/138/P